Where Do I Come From?

Claire Rayner

Arlington Books
King Street, St. James's
London SW1

WHERE DO I COME FROM?
First published 1974
this edition published 1987 by
Arlington Books (Publishers) Ltd
15–17 King Street, St. James's
London SW1

Reprinted 1988

© Claire Rayner 1974

Typeset by Wordbook Ltd, London
Printed and bound by
Richard Clay Ltd, Suffolk

British Library Cataloguing in Publication Data

Rayner, Claire
Where do I come from? – 2nd ed.
1. Sex instruction for children
I. Title
612'.6   HQ53

ISBN 0–85140–714–5

Contents

For Parents

1   Why? How? When?

Why?

Why is it necessary to have yet another book on the subject of sex education? After all, the whole spectrum of sex education has become part of the syllabus in many schools and there has been a positive rash of books, articles, television and radio programmes, and newspaper discussions on the subject. Surely we can forget the whole boring business *now?*

In fact we can't, partly because it is, despite all the widespread discussion, far from being boring (anyone who retains the merest spark of human sexuality, which is virtually everyone at every age, is interested in the workings of human sexuality) and partly because every new year there arrives yet another new generation thirsting for knowledge, information and advice. The subject of sex education is thus of constant interest, and in constant need of rethinking.

While it is true that essentially people remain

much the same, there is little doubt that social attitudes towards important human activities are always changing. Just think of the difference between Victorian teachings heavily based on the theme 'Thou shalt not, because it's dirty but if you can't help it, then certainly thou shalt not enjoy it' and the contemporary 'Sex is nice and meant to be a pleasure' approach. Consider, too, our changing views of the reproductive side of sex. It isn't all that long since a woman who appeared on a radio quiz show and announced that she had 10 children would be greeted by a hearty round of approving applause; but let her make the same statement today, and the chances are that in most parts of the country she'd be met by lip-pursing disapproval. The biblical injunction to 'be fruitful and multiply' has diminishing relevance in a planet as overcrowded as ours has become; one in real danger of being destroyed by the pollution created by over population.

So that is the first answer to the question 'Why?' But there are other 'why' questions to be asked. Why teach children about sex at all? Plenty of people will say it's totally unnecessary, that sex is a natural part of being human and that children when they grow up will be able to take part in sexual activity without being taught, just as they are able to breathe and eat and later to walk and run without being taught. Up to a point of course, this is true. Sex *is* natural, and expressions of sexuality *are* instinctive, but that doesn't mean to say that all children will automatically grow up able to obey their instincts — and the reason is that they may suffer what could be called 'negative' sex education.

Children reared by people who refuse to talk about sex at all (for whatever reason) and who therefore don't get the chance to express their natural interest in their developing bodies inevitably get feelings of fear about sex. What *is* this mysterious thing that is so interesting, so powerful in the feelings it creates, and yet which may not be talked about? It must be something very dreadful to be so hedged about in secrecy, the young mind reasons.

Out of this fear comes guilt — because afraid or not, repressed or not, children will always have an interest in sex — and out of guilt comes anxiety. And these three feelings together can totally destroy an adult's ability to respond to his or her normal instincts. All over this country — all over the world, for that matter — there are people whose normal sexuality has been so distorted by bad sex education that they are totally incapable of getting normal pleasure from their own humanity. At best they are personally unhappy; at worst, they are driven to seek sexual satisfactions in ways that are destructive to other people as well as themselves. People who commit sex crimes — from the most minor form of 'breach of peace' exhibitionism to the horror of murder — are not born wicked. All too often they are the product of bad education, and sex education is very much part of that process.

If you want to go into the subject of sex education at an even deeper level, consider the political and financial implications (and there are some, strange as it may sound). Because the rewards of happy sexuality are so very enjoyable it isn't beyond the bounds of possibility that a Government could develop techniques to discourage people enjoying sex, only allowing them to find relief from their sexual frustrations as a reward for being 'good citizens'. That may sound like science-fiction — but so many things we take for granted (contraception for example, or fertility drugs) would have seemed even more incredible to our great grandparents.

Certainly there can be financial aspects; the people who make vast sums of money from selling pornographic books, magazines and films thrive best in a society where sex education aims at repressing individuals and filling them with disgust and shame at their own normal procedures. People who are made to feel like that are ripe to become customers for the back-street satisfactions that hard pornography provides.

Every reader of this book will have his or her own ideas about why sex education is needed for their children; it would be an impertinence for anyone else to try to force other views on them. However, many people find help in formulating their own ideas by considering those of others, so for them the next paragraphs will offer my own answer to the question 'Why teach children about sex?' (I am not for one moment suggesting that this is the only possible answer; just that it might help you to assess your own attitudes more easily if you have the basis of someone else's to work on.)

I believe that human sexuality operates on at least two levels. Firstly, there is purely the biological one, in which it is linked to reproduction. This function human sex shares with animal sex at all levels, from the merest of newts up to the most advanced of the great apes.

It is in the second function that our humanity most clearly displays itself. In this function sex is both an expression of love and a creation of it — and don't ask me to define love, that abstract complexity of feelings which drive all of us throughout most of our lives; philosophers, poets and artists have been trying to do that since man first stood up on his hind legs, and haven't fully succeeded yet — and also a form of *re*-creation. Sex has been described as the 'most popular human sport' and this is true. And never think calling it a sport is to diminish it; without recreation and entertainment and the stimulation these things bring, most humans would shrivel up and could even die, for such stimulation is as vital to human life as food and warmth.

How?

When it comes to teaching children the purely biological side of sex, there is little need to worry.

As long as a child lives among humans, and observes their activities he or she will be able to fulfil the reproductive side of sexuality. Certainly the female of the species will. She only has to be there, need take no active part at all, in order to conceive. The male, of course, has to be rather more active, and there is no doubt that some males are inhibited in their adult sexual function, as far as reproduction is concerned, because of bad sex education in childhood. There are men who are totally incapable of achieving an erection when with a woman, and even more incapable of carrying intercourse to the completion necessary if they are to father children, simply because they have been so filled with alarm, disgust and fear of their normal processes that they are sexually paralysed in any direct confrontation with the opposite sex.

However, as I say, it isn't difficult to teach children hard physical facts (in the second part of this book, I outline them for those readers who are a bit unsure of them, even though they're adults and parents — and that, I assure you is the situation of an enormous number of people in our society) because facts are so easy.

What is difficult is getting the emotional part right, the part that deals with the second use of human sex. Because, for us, sex is so much more than mere reproduction even talking about the scientific facts becomes a matter filled with feeling. The person who can discuss in a truly cool, emotionally uninvolved manner what happens when a man and woman meet in sexual encounter is a rare creature indeed. I don't think he can even exist. Whether he shows it or not, knows it or not, he is emotionally stirred in some way by thinking and talking about what happens.

This means that when people talk about sex they are conveying far more than mere information-filled words. They are putting across a whole attitude.

You can prove this for yourself. Take a sample sentence to do with sex, for example, 'People are sexual'. This is a cold statement of fact with which no one can argue. People *do* exist in two genders, and *do* use sex to reproduce themselves. Whether you think sex is nice or nasty, good or bad, funny or sacred, important or trivial, it is *so*.

Now say these three words aloud several times in a different tone of voice. Say it with pleasure, say it with disgust. Say it as a question, say it as an answer. Say it as though you were in a church and say it as though it were a huge joke. Say it with a smutty giggle, say it with scientific detachment. You see how easily three words conveying a fact can also convey a whole range of complex feelings?

It is this that parents who are wondering about the sex education of their children need to get clear first and foremost.

Before even considering the children you have to consider yourself and your own knowledge and attitudes.

If you are one of the unhappy people of this world who regard sex as horrible, dirty, 'animal like' and so on, then quite honestly I don't think you should attempt to do any direct teaching at all. Leave it to someone else who has a more relaxed attitude — perhaps a schoolteacher — and hope that you won't pass on to your children your own unfortunately warped point of view.

If on the other hand, you enjoy holding the happy point of view which starts from the assumption that children should know about sex in order that they may be happy about their own human normality; may be able in adult life to make satisfying relationships, and may be able to fit into society in a way that makes someone else, as well as themselves, comfortable, then you have few problems. Whether you know it or not you have since your children's birth been teaching them in the best possible way about sex.

You have been handling them physically with affection and gentleness based on your own pleasure in your physical contacts with your spouse. I am not assuming, as so many people do, that only mothers are interested in teaching their children about sex: I'm taking it for granted that plenty of fathers will want to read this book. In your contacts with each other as lovers, you have been giving yourselves in your roles as parents an inner sense of satisfaction, a self-esteem, that you have been passing on to your children. Whenever a man kisses his wife, whenever a woman hugs her husband and their children see them they share the warmth and security of their parents' love for each other. They take it for granted, these fortunate children, that loving physical contact between a man and a woman is a good, happy and above all normal thing.

This doesn't mean to say that you need be agitated if sometimes you and your partner have arguments, find sex less than perfect, experience periods of depression and an associated lack of interest in sex. Such experiences are part of everyday living, and it would be unrealistic in the extreme to pretend that the 'normal' family is one that is always wrapped in sweetness and light, where the father never goes out of the house in a rage, having forgotten to kiss his wife goodbye, and the mother never loses her temper and bursts into tears. Let me make it very clear indeed that in talking of the example parents set their children I am referring to basic feeling, not mere surface behaviour. There can be families where rows never happen and everyone is always exceedingly courteous — even affectionate — to each other, but underneath flows a river of coldness and rejection; just as there can be families where there's at least one argument a day, but which is based on warm love and acceptance of each others' frailties. Normal loving people have arguments, normal loving people have occasional sexual difficulties, normal loving people get attacks of the miseries — *And they bring up their children perfectly successfully*. Children will have to live as adults in a warm, human, imperfect world, and the best training for such adult life is living with warm, human, imperfect parents.

However, there are families in which the arguments, the occasional flashes of temper and the periods of depression are more than superficial expressions of exasperation with the day-to-day difficulties of life, inevitable to people facing financial problems, job problems, housework problems, family problems. There are marriages in which there is a deep sexual unease between the partners, an unease with which they have been unable to come to terms.

Sometimes it may happen that a woman is deeply disappointed. She may be one of those who do not enjoy much in the way of sexual feelings, find intercourse rather tedious, and can't understand why so many people fuss about it so; for them it is something to be tolerated, not enjoyed. It is difficult for such women, in their roles as mothers, to teach their children that sex is a happy joyful thing; how can they when as far as they are concerned it's so drearily boring?

Similarly, there are men who are disappointed in their sex lives, who cannot find the fulfilment they have always wanted, who regard home as a place to escape from, rather than to, and seek sexual satisfaction with other women, rather than with their own wives. Such a man in his role as father is obviously not going to be able to teach his children what real love between a man and woman can and should be at its ideal best.

Does this mean that the children of such marriages

have no hope of gaining the sort of sex education that will enable them to enjoy better and more satisfying permanent relationships when they grow up?

It need not — as long as the parents face the fact that they have a problem and do something about solving it. And in fact, this happens in a great many families. It is when the children start to show signs of being interested in sexuality, start asking searching questions, that the parents for the first time admit that they need to sort out their own ideas.

It isn't all that difficult to get help in adjusting an unsatisfactory sexual relationship. Many of the problems with which people struggle on in grim silence could be solved fairly quickly, if only the sufferers would seek expert help. A woman who avoids intercourse because it causes her more discomfort than pleasure could well find, if she sees a doctor, that she is suffering from a small physical problem that once put right could lead to a much happier experience for her. A woman who is unable to enjoy her own sexuality because she fears becoming pregnant again can often be reassured enough to gain new pleasure from her marriage after she discusses contraception with an expert.

Yet all too often, people are too shy to see a doctor or go to a clinic. How stupid this is! If they had a boil on a leg that made walking painful, they'd seek help for that, even regard such help as their right; why not see a sexual difficulty in the same way? It is the same as the boil, if it's causing pain and limits activity. The sufferers have the same right to have the disorder dealt with.

So a vital step on the road to successful sex education for your child is honest discussion of your sex life with each other. If there are any problems, bring them out into the daylight and *talk* about them (and if you are close enough to share physical sex, then you are close enough to talk about it; too often couples are too shy to put their needs and feelings into words — yet they must if they are really to find the happiness they want) and then, if you can't cope by yourself, seek expert help. At the end of this book there are addresses of useful advisory organisations that will be of help.

When?

It is about this question that many parents agonise the most. What is the right age to tell a child about the mechanics of child birth, what periods are, what intercourse is about, what VD is, about contraception, abortion, homosexuality and so on? Can they be told too young? Is there a proper time at which a child should be taken on one side and told the 'facts of life'?

The simple answer to this question is 'Leave it to the child'. Children are, by definition, question-asking machines. They are like explorers thrown on to the shore of a totally strange continent, needing to find out as much as they can as fast as they can.

They start asking questions as soon as they can talk. 'Why?, 'What's that?, 'What's that for?', and so on.

If the family has a basically happy attitude to sexuality, questions about sex will come mixed up with all the others. A two year old girl watching her father undress will point to his penis and testicles and say 'What's that?' A boy of the same age will see his mother in the bath and point at her breasts and say, 'What are they?' (and very amusing sometimes can their own ideas on the answer be. My own small son at two and a half added approvingly, 'I like them. Did you knit them?')

And all the parents have to do is answer the question that is asked. The child of this age is busily seeking labels for everything, and there is no special sexual significance in his wish to know the names of these objects any more than there is in the wish to know the names of aeroplanes, trains or anything else.

Some parents may prefer to label the sexual parts of the body with nicknames or pet names (that they often use themselves in love-making) and though this is a very popular thing to do, there is something to be said for using the real words. There is nothing intrinsically 'rude' or bad in a word, after all; saying 'That is my penis' is as acceptable to a child as saying 'That is my winkle' or whatever; and the drawback to pet names and nicknames is that sooner or later the child will meet the real words and may be bewildered. So, just as few people today think it necessary to tell a child a horse is called a 'gee-gee', a train a 'puff-puff' or a dog a 'woof-woof', knowing the child can learn the real word just as easily, neither is it necessary to babify sexual words.

Some children ask immediately, 'What's it for?' Others don't. If they don't fair enough. No need to say another thing. The child will ask when he or she is ready. And when the question does come, a simple direct answer is all that is needed. A girl may be fascinated to know that her father pees through his penis, and may settle for that, just as her brother will probably settle at first for being told the name of his mother's strange (strange to him because he doesn't have them) appendages. But the likelihood is that the child will ask more about 'What is it for?' — *as long as the climate is right*. Do remember that any hint of parental embarrassment or tension can be enough to give the child, however young, an unspoken warning to lay off. Never forget that children are very accurate barometers of their parents' moods. They know when their questions are taboo.

If the child doesn't ask this follow-on question on one of the later occasions when the question is asked again (and as every parent knows, asking a question once is never enough; every child asks the same questions over and over — *ad nauseam!*) there is no harm in adding comfortably, 'It's for making babies as well,' or 'They're for feeding babies'.

Since all children — like all adults — are totally fascinated by anything that has any relevance to themselves, the usual effect of such a statement is to release a small flood of eager questions, along the 'how' lines. And once again, the sensible parent answers each question that is asked, but no more. It is never wise to push more information at a child than they are ready for. By all means stimulate him to ask a question by making a simple statement, but if the question does not come, leave it at that. It will eventually!

You will remember we are here talking about the questions asked by very young children. Given the opportunity, two and three year olds *will* ask questions about adult body structure and can cope with the answers. And having asked those questions and been given interesting answers — not the sort that close the door firmly after them, but which leave it invitingly ajar for more questions — the child will go on and on seeking and absorbing information.

Using this technique a child can start school at the age of five knowing a great deal: that men and women are made differently; that all grown-ups used to be children; that all children used to be babies; that all babies grew inside their mothers' bellies; that all mothers were given half of the tiny parts that grow into babies by fathers; that all fathers put their share of baby-making parts into the mother through the baby-hole in her body called a vagina; that these parts were made in his testicles, and came out through his penis; that the new baby comes out of his mother the same way he got in; and that after he was born, he got the milk to make him grow from his mother's breasts. Altogether a great deal of fascinating information, easily and gradually obtained in the same way the child learned about the sky and the ground, flowers and trees, eating and drinking, and everything else in this exciting world — by asking his parents and being given simple answers.

The great thing about telling these very little children the story of reproduction in this way is that there is so little shyness about it. However relaxed and happy about their adult sexuality parents may be, however open-minded and relaxed they are, it is always easiest to talk to little children about sex because they do not yet have strong sexual feelings. Of course, they have some (just watch a baby feeding at the breast, nuzzling and mouthing — he is clearly finding sensual pleasure in it, and so he should, for that is what life is all about) but they are not specific. Later, as the child moves into puberty (see p 31) his natural interest in sex will become very much more particular; a part of his own feelings as his body grows. At this stage there may well be a natural sexual tension between adult and child in talking of sex. But there is none of this in the little child, and learning about reproduction in the same way he learns about everything else is what makes it in his eyes what it is supposed to be — the most natural thing in the world.

It is later that other questions will come up, questions about menstruation, for example. An under-five can't cope with that subject nearly as easily as with stories of how babies are made, for babyhood fascinates the little child; he is still so very near his own! But later on a girl especially learns to relate herself more closely to her mother, and is very interested to think about the way she will herself one day be like her.

When a seven or eight year old is given the chance to see her mother's menstrual protection (say being with her at the chemist when she buys towels or tampons) she is also given the chance to ask what these things are and what they are for. And since she already knows about baby-making, she can be told about the processes of menstruation in a very easily understood way. Boys, too, should be told about menstruation, of course, for the idea that girls should learn only about female anatomy and physiology and boys only about males and never the twain shall meet is patently absurd. Boys can be encouraged to ask in the way girls are — and lucky the boy who has sisters; so much easier to get the questions going in a mixed gender family.

As the children grow older, they incorporate more and more of their knowledge into their own lives. By the time they reach the end of childhood as such — ten, eleven, twelve — they begin to be ready to talk about other aspects of sex. Newspaper and TV news stories will often encourage them to talk of and ask questions about such matters as contraception, abortion and VD.

What parents tell a child on these matters depends heavily on their own moral, religious and political attitudes. Some families believe in the use of contraception and for them the answers to the child's questions about it are in approving terms, explaining that mothers could have a baby a year if parents did not prevent extra births, that people make love out of love as well as because they want babies. Those who believe that over-large families are not to be admired may use the opportunity to discuss with their children the whys and wherefores of their beliefs and also the opinions of those people who hold the opposite point of view. They will see to it that the children are encouraged to give their opinions too. Altogether, this can be a great opportunity to discuss not only contraception but a whole range of human and social responsibilities. And if a family does not believe in the use of contraception, the children have a right to know why not, and to be told the views of the opposition in just the same way. This is how sex education becomes education in the true sense of the word.

Later in this book a good deal of straight factual information is offered on VD, contraceptive methods, homosexuality etc. Parents reading this may either choose to talk to their children on the subject or prefer to give this book to the older child to read for himself. In order not to intrude too much on the parental need to offer moral and social views of their own on these subject I have made this information as

neutral as I can, offering facts rather than opinions —
with the exception of the section on homosexuality,
where I undoubtedly offer a moral judgment.

We now know so much more about the so-called
sexual deviations that I believe it would be very
wrong of any writer on this subject not to offer today's generally tolerant point of view, so you will not
find homosexuality labelled as 'perversion' in these
pages, for in common with the majority of informed
people, I do not regard it in this light. Homosexuals
may have a different attitude to sex than most people,
but that doesn't make them 'worse' than most people
any more than it makes them 'better'. They are just
different. I hope that even parents who have a deep
distaste for the subject and who were themselves
reared to see this aspect of human sexual behaviour
as 'evil' will be able to allow themselves the chance
to think again about it.

At what age should this more complex material
be talked about? Once again, ideally at the age the
child asks, whatever that age may be. However,
one has to take into account the child himself. Some
are avidly interested in the world about them, read
newspapers and watch news broadcasts; others don't.
For this latter group, it will be necessary to introduce
the subjects. I believe this should not be left until
the child is well into adult life (as it so often was
in the past, when people could reach adulthood and
be married before they even know of the existence
of birth control or diseases or any of these subjects

under review) but that the child should be equipped with knowledge early. And it is worth remembering that just as it is emotionally more comfortable to talk about conception and birth with the very young children, so it is emotionally more comfortable to talk about these other complex subjects with children before they are themselves emotionally involved. So, I would say that by the age of twelve or thirteen children should be told.

How? The direct question, again, I believe, but this time it may have to come from the parent. 'Do you know about contraception?' is a good starter. Some parents may be startled to find that the children already know a great deal, because they have been told at school in sex education classes, but haven't mentioned the matter at home. If this is so, then it's a good chance for a parent to encourage the child to talk about it — for easy family conversations are always to be encouraged and anyway, the child may have got the information a bit wrong, it does happen. (It can also happen that the child can tell the parents something they didn't know!) A follow up question from you — 'What did they tell you? I'd love to know' is perfectly reasonable.

There then, is a brief rundown of the ideal way in which a child is taught. To recapitulate, his questions are answered as they arise, from the age of two onwards (as soon as he/she can talk, in other words) and the child is stimulated gently to ask questions if necessary — but information is *never* forced upon him. When a child reaches the age of eight or so if questions about periods have not yet been asked, an attempt should be made to stimulate such questions — and this is as necessary for boys as girls (and though obviously you can take a little more time with a boy he shouldn't reach his own puberty without being told about periods; he'll reach puberty at around twelve to thirteen or so). It's worth remembering, by the way, that boys at mixed-sex schools will hear something of the subject before boys at one-sex schools because of mixed sex-education classes, as well as greater contact with girls).

Using this method a relaxed comfortable family will find their children are very well informed on the mechanics of sex by the age of puberty, and are therefore well prepared for it. The child will also have been given in the easiest and most natural way possible a view of sexual morality that is based on the example he or she has seen at home. If you want to rear children who will enter loving, lifelong, one-partner relationships in which they can happily rear their own children, then the best way to teach them is to enjoy such a life yourself.

The Parent Alone

Parents who have had unhappy personal experiences should not despair at reading this. You may be a widow or a widower, a divorced woman, an unmarried mother rearing your own child alone or a man whose wife has left him, coping with your family unaided, but you can still give your children a healthy view of adult sexuality as long as you have the courage and honesty to talk about your own situation to your children as they pass through childhood and early adolescence. They will need to be told as directly as you can, and with a minimum of bitterness and mud-slinging, why you are alone. If your marriage failure is due to a breakdown in communication say so — and admit where you went wrong yourself. If you are an unmarried mother by choice (and plenty of women are these days) then your child is entitled to know why you made that choice.

If you are alone because of death, then it is perhaps easier to talk of the absent parent's sexual role with tenderness, as it should be discussed, but you need to be aware of one special difficulty you may have to face. If the parent who had an unhappy experience must avoid the trap of bitterness the widow/widower must avoid the trap of over-idealising the absent parent. To make a dead mother or father sound like an angel incarnate may set a child an impossible model, and cause such a sense of inability to 'measure up' that the child in his/her own adult life never takes the risk of getting sexually involved with anyone for fear of 'failure'.

But having said all this, do remember that as long as there is one loving parent, a child can grow to have a happy adult sexuality of his own, even if the other parent is absent or less loving than might be. I have in these pages described an 'ideal' family setup, but I am the first to agree that not every family can be so ideally constituted. The single parent will obviously find it takes more effort to rear children successfully — but perhaps it is more rewarding.

Late Starters

Some readers at this stage will be feeling very frustrated indeed, since they picked up this book because their children have reached the age of ten or twelve or fifteen or so. What is the good of discussing what they *should* have done when the child was a baby? It is *now* that matters.

If you have reacted as so many parents have reacted in the past, and tried to keep sex in a separate compartment of your life and so have never discussed the matter without your children at all, then of course it's not going to be easy for you. But don't assume your child knows nothing. That is very unlikely, unless you live in a totally remote island where your child has no contact with other people. Children talk to each other, to other adults, watch television shows, read magazines and papers and generally absorb a lot of information. Your problem may be not so much deciding what to tell them that they need to know, as discovering what it is they know that is inaccurate (unfortunately many children get the facts very mixed up when they pick them up in this casual way) and where the gaps in their collection of 'facts of life' may be.

I think the easiest way to do this is to be straight-forward with your child 'I should have talked to you about sex long ago, but I never quite got round to it', is a fair beginning. You may be surprised at how offhand your children are in response. 'Oh, we've done all that at school' — or 'Oh, I know all about *that*' — is a very common answer. Some parents are so deeply relieved at this that they say gratefully, 'Fine!' and forget all about it. I don't think that's altogether wise. First of all he may not know 'all about it' at all, but be embarrassed and trying to put you off; or, as was said earlier, he could have got it all wrong anyway.

So, perseverance is needed and this book can provide a method for you. The ensuing pages offer a detailed account of how children's bodies change, during puberty, into those of mature adult men and women; how those men and women function; how together they make babies; how those babies develop in the mother's body, are born, and are fed after birth.

Because this information is designed to be read not only by adults but by children around the age of puberty the language is simple but the facts are as direct and as complete as it is possible for them to be in the confines of this small book. Once the child has read it, you can ask him what he thought about it; whether the information is the same as that he already had, whether he feels there is more he wants to know, and so on. Used as a jumping-off point for discussion in this way it can help parents who do not easily talk about sex to find a common ground with their developing children.

And if you are so completely tongue-tied about sex that you find it almost impossible to talk about it to your own husband or wife, let alone to your children, then let this second section of the book do your talking for you. You are far from being alone if you feel like this, and no amount of nagging along the lines of 'It's a parent's duty to talk to their children about sex' is going to make you any the less tongue-tied; in fact it will only add a burden of miserable guilt to your underlying embarrassment. If you are shy, then you're shy; if you were brought up to be tongue-tied, then that's all there is to it. Sex education for your children is not the arena in which to set about trying to change your personality! Your children will come to no harm if you make the effort to set the physical facts in front of them, and will benefit even more if you can tell them who they can talk to on personal matters if they ever want to. Many schools these days provide counselling services for their pupils — someone the children can talk to confidentially when they feel the need — and even those that don't usually have at least one member of the staff who is approachable on the subject of sex education. Aim your child at these teachers, provide him with adequate reading matter and just go on loving him in your own quiet way. You may not be one of the world's great talkers, but you are his or her loving parent, and that matters more than the most fluent of chat.

2 The Physical Facts

What Happens To Children

If you look at a naked little boy and a naked little girl standing with their backs to you, you can't tell, for sure, which is which. They both have the same shape, and they are both smooth, with hair growing only on their heads. When they speak, they both have the same high treble note to their voices. Even from the front they don't look all that different; both have flat chests with a pair of pink 'pimples' on them, both have round slightly sticking-out bellies. It is only when you look at their surface sex organs that you can detect the difference between them. (Fig. 1)

Between the groins — the place where the legs meet the body — a little girl has what appears to be a slit, and the little boy a small thumb-like knob of soft tissue, with behind it a pouch made of wrinkled skin which is a slightly darker pink in colour than the surrounding skin.

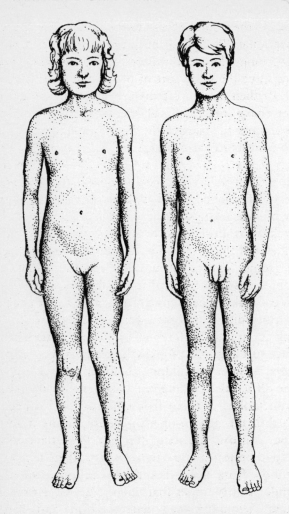

Fig 1. Boys and girls look much the same.

Inside their bodies these two children are still very much alike. They both have the same sort of brain, heart, lungs, kidneys, muscles and joints and bones. They have the same sort of blood and gastric juices, and all their body systems work in the same way. They have the same glands producing chemical messengers to instruct the body how to grow and how to react to various experiences. It is only in their internal sex organs they are a bit different; inside a girl there is a tiny muscular organ called the *uterus* (the old fashioned word was *womb*) together with a pair of special egg-making organs called *ovaries*. The boy also has special seed-making organs; his are called *testicles* and they are inside that little pouch between the groins. The pouch is called the *scrotum* and the knob of tissue in front of it is called the *penis*.

We all take it very much for granted that children are quite different from adults, but if you stop to think about it the difference is really very remarkable. it isn't just a matter of growth; if adults were merely bigger versions of children, then you would have the same difficulty in telling one naked one from another if you looked at them from the rear. Of course, it isn't difficult; grown-up women are a quite different shape to grown-up men. (Fig. 2) They have round hips and bottoms, and narrow waists; their arms stick out more from their sides; they tend to be softer and rounder and plumper than men. Men have broader, squarer shoulders and narrow hips and flattish bottoms, and are usually not nearly as smooth as

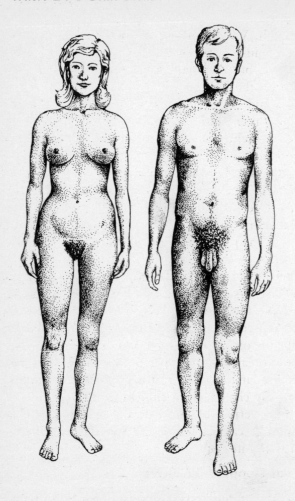

Fig 2. Men and women are very different to look at.

women. Women have hair on their bodies — across the groins, between the legs, and under the arms, usually, but men have it not only in these places but also on their chests, their bellies, lots of it on their arms and legs, and most noticeably, on their faces. When men and women talk, it is usually quite obvious which is which; men have deeper voices than women.

Why are there these differences, and how do they happen? They exist because men and women have two different jobs to do when it comes to making new human beings. Both of them have to produce half of the parts that start the baby growing, but one of them — the woman — also has to provide a place where the baby can develop and grow big enough to have a separate life of its own. Also she has to provide food for the baby for the first few weeks of that separate life. On pages 56 and 57 there is an explanation of how men and women together set about creating a new person, and how that persons grows. First, however, it is important to understand how the change from child to adult happens.

The period of time during which the changes appear is called *puberty* and it is rather different in boys and in girls.

What Happens To Boys

The age of puberty varies very much from individual to individual. Some boys will show signs of the start at around eleven or so; others not until they are thirteen or older. There is no virtue in reaching puberty earlier or anything wrong in starting later — though unfortunately some boys do get agitated when they see their friends all going into puberty while they seem to lag behind. There's no need for them to get agitated, however. Everyone gets there sooner or later.

At whatever age it starts then, it is heralded fairly obviously by a sudden spurt in growth. Children don't grow at an even rate but in fits and starts; they may not grow an inch all summer, and then suddenly shoot up three inches between the start of the autumn term and the beginning of the Christmas holidays. The spurt that comes before puberty is a very big one. Some boys have suddenly grown as much as six inches taller during a few months, which is startling for them and disconcerting for people around them.

It is at this stage that some boys who have been plump suddenly shed their excess weight, and become rather 'gangly'. They tend to look bony about the wrists, knees and ankles, and sometimes the jaw. (This look is often accentuated by the way clothes are worn the wrong sizes. No one blames parents for being unwilling to keep buying complete new wardrobes for a boy who is sprouting faster than a mushroom, but it does help the boy's self esteem if he can have at least one outfit in which he looks as though he belongs).

What is happening at this stage is that bones are

grower bigger as well as longer. The male has more muscle power than the female (very much needed when humans were a hunting species which required such power to ensure survival) and strong muscles demand strong bones to support them.

Another interesting area of growth is in the boy's neck — in his larynx, the organ of the voice. This too grows larger, and may become more prominent, sticking out low in the front of the neck, where it is called the Adam's apple. (There's a myth which says that when Adam ate the apple Eve gave him in Paradise it choked him, so men are said to have carried the lump there ever since. It's a nice story, but that is all it is. It is no more true than the myth that men have one rib less than women 'because God used one of Adam's to make Eve'. Men and women have the same number of ribs on both sides.) The effect of this growth is a change in the pitch of the voice, and because the growth is so rapid, lots of boys have trouble in learning how to adapt to it. That is why some boys find that while they are speaking, their usual treble voice has taken an embarrassing swoop to a lower huskier note and vice versa. People who tease boys when this happens are thoughtless, for such teasing can cause a lot of distress. (It is hard to say why this change comes in puberty; perhaps in pre-historic times the male of the species needed a deep strong voice to use for calling to hunting colleagues? It's a suggestion — but it could be as wrong as the Adam's apple myth.)

At the same time, the skin starts to change. Just as the roundness of childhood gives way to the muscularity of young adulthood, so does the smooth childish skin give way to a coarser hairier one. Some boys make the change very easily, but others suffer that bane of the young years — spots and blackheads. It has to be said that some families are specially plagued by it, and generation after generation of its young men (and women) are made miserable by acne of face and back. (On page 84 there is an account of some methods of dealing with this common problem.)

The hairiness, of course, is not a problem. Many boys are enchanted by the first sprouting of facial hair and set about regular shaving with great pleasure. (It is interesting to note by the way that it is the practice of shaving that makes facial hair in men coarse and stiff to the touch; If the hair is never cut it develops into a very silky moustache and beard.)

Other parts of the body get hairy, too. Under the arms, across the belly, and round the sex organs. The degree to which it grows depends on the texture of the hair, which is an inherited characteristic — some families have soft fine hair, others coarser thicker hair — and the boy's colouring. A dark haired boy will obviously show the growth more than a blonde.

It is worth making three points here for boys who are anxious about their hair growth. Firstly, it takes some years for a full male hair growth pattern to be established — it is not until the boy is well into his twenties or even later that it can be said to be complete; secondly, that some men never grow hair on their chests at all; and thirdly, and this is the most important of all, hairiness is not an index of masculinity. You can't say that a man with a lot of body hair is more manly than a smoother person. It just isn't true.

Another obvious change the boy notices is that his sex organs start to grow. The scrotum and its enclosed testicles become larger and heavier; the penis grows both longer and thicker. Also, the skin covering the penis, and that of the scrotum may tend to darken in colour somewhat — this depends on basic skin colouring, and doesn't always happen.

These are the obvious changes in the boy's anatomy — the way his body is made. Before going on to look at changes in physiology — the way the body works — it would be useful to know why all these changes happen.

It will be remembered that both boys and girls have a number of special glands which produce chemical messengers called hormones to tell the body how to grow and behave. These are the *endocrine* glands and include the *hypothalamus* and its close companion the *pituitary* which lie deep at the base of the brain; the *thyroid*, which wraps itself around the voice box at the root of the neck; the *adrenals* which are just over each of the kidneys and the *testicles* in boys. There are others, but they are not important here.

When a boy reaches the body weight that triggers

the endocrine system (which explains why some thin boys start puberty a little later than some bigger ones) the glands start to work. The hypothalamus and the pituitary are the leaders of the team — they've been described as the 'conductors of the orchestra', telling all the others what to do and when to do it. They get *their* control from the brain. The brain itself gets its information from all over the body, so it's really a circular system.

The hypothalamus and the pituitary instruct the thyroid, which is involved with the rate at which food and oxygen are burnt up in the body. They also instruct the adrenals, which have a great many jobs; the transport of food, salts and fluids around the body; growth processes, and, very importantly, the creation of those special sexual characteristics — hairiness, skin texture and body shape — we've already been looking at. Finally, instructions go to the testicles to start their development.

The testicles have a double job; not only do they produce special hormones dealing with growth and sexual function; they also produce the actual cells that will be needed in due course to create new human beings. These cells are called *spermatozoa* or *sperm* for short. When a baby boy is born there lies deep within his tiny testicles all the potential for making the many millions of sperm he will need during his lifetime. At the time of puberty the machinery for creating these sperm is 'switched on' and as the testicles grow, so they start to produce them.

These cells look very much like tadpoles. Each sperm is very small, but each carries half the cells needed to make a baby. And each carries the message which will make either a girl or boy baby for it is the *father* who decides the sex of a child, not the mother. They carry in their head part all the information to make a new baby and are equipped with a whippy tail that will help them to swim towards a female's egg cell — more about that on pages 56 and 60. Right now we will stay with the testicles (Fig. 3).

There are other glands near to the testicles also involved with what is going on. Just as the testicles produce sperm, so do they produce a special liquid substance in which the sperm will live. The sperm and the liquid together are stored in a special sac

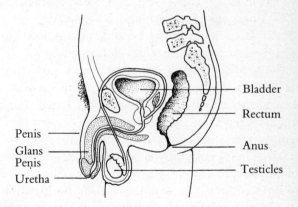

Penis
Glans
Penis
Uretha

Bladder
Rectum
Anus
Testicles

Fig. 3. The male sex organs are almost entirely on the surface of the body.

just behind the penis. There the *semen* (the name of
the sperm and liquid together) will stay until it is
'thrown' out of the body. When this does happen
it will pass along the tube which runs through the
middle of the penis. This tube has two jobs. Not
only does it carry semen when it wants to leave the
body, but also urine — waste water — from the
nearby bladder.

There are a number of other important things to
know about the penis. It is more than just a fleshy
tube; the tissue of which it is made is rather like a
sponge. When the sponge part is not being used the
penis is a soft little organ that hangs down from the
body. But sometimes, under special circumstances,
all the sponge-like cells of the penis fill with blood
and become distended. This has the remarkable effect
of making the penis temporarily become very hard
and erect and a much larger size so that is stands
away from the body at a sharp angle. The reason for
this remarkable ability will be understood when we
go on to look at how the adult male body actually
works. But a little more information about the penis
at this point; at the top of it there is a cap called the
glans penis which ends in a narrow ridge. This is
covered with a flap of skin which is called the *prepuce*
or *foreskin*. This has the special job of protecting the
very sensitive glans penis. Although it does have this
job to do it has long been a practice among many
people to remove it. To do this an operation called
circumcision is performed. It means, quite literally,

'round cutting' and the top of the flap is snipped off and the remains are pushed back behind the ridge. Most societies which practice this operation as a routine do it for religious and ritual reasons, but it can sometimes be done for medical reasons. In a few cases the foreskin is rather tight and causes a blockage at the end of the penis, so that urine cannot escape easily.

For sometime now circumcision has been fashionable in this country, with parents deciding to have a baby boy circumcised almost as soon as he is born just in case there are medical problems later on. When you add this number to those who have the operation done for religious reasons you see why many boys find when they see each other's bare penises in shower

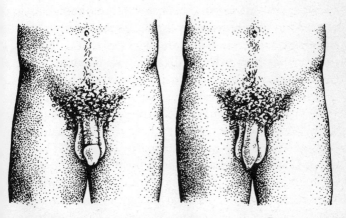

Fig. 4. The boy on the left has been circumcised; the boy on the right has not.

rooms at school that there appear to be two different types. In fact there aren't; it's simply that some have had the operation and some have not. (Fig. 4)

Something else boys may sometimes notice in shower rooms is the way some boys seem to have much bigger scrotums and testicles than others. There are two possible reasons. Firstly, the testicles develop deep inside the body before birth and descend just before birth or not long afterwards to come out of a small gap in the muscle floor of the belly to get into the scrotum. Sometimes this descent isn't complete in the baby, and the testicle therefore 'wanders', sometimes going back through the little gap in the muscle to be inside the body and sometimes coming down. In cases where the testicles refuse to come down at all it may be necessary for the boy to have a small operation to ensure that they are brought to the surface of the body. They can't work properly unless they are. Obviously a boy with undescended testicles will look small around the scrotum.

Secondly it may sometimes appear that the scrotum and testicles are very small because of the way the scrotum is very responsive to changes in temperature. If a boy is warm and relaxed the scrotum lies fairly low, holding the testicles well away from the body. But when he's cold, the scrotum will wrinkle up tightly and bring the testicles much closer to his groins. In this position obviously it will all look much smaller. There is a very good reason for this reaction. If the testicles are to do their job properly they have to be kept at a temperature of around 95°F – but this is rather lower than normal body heat which tends to be about 98°F or so. So, when the body is particularly warm, the scrotum relaxes to allow the testicles to go further away from the source of heat. But then if the temperature drops much below the ideal 95°F, the scrotum brings the testicles back up to the warmth of the body so that they will be protected.

With all this information about the physical equipment a boy has we can now go on to look at how it all works.

Once the testicles set about their job of producing ripe sperm they work pretty well continuously. They don't just produce enough to fill the storage sac and then stop. This means that every so often the body will have a need to throw out the collected sperm in order to make room for fresh supplies to be stored. This usually happens for the very first time during the night while a boy is asleep, and a popular name for this experience is a *wet dream*. The boy wakes suddenly to discover he's damp and sticky. He may just remember having had a very exciting dream in which he was involved with a girl (or boy come to that) or in other ways was sexually busy. Unless the boy has been told of the possibility of a *nocturnal emission* which is the proper name for a wet dream, he may become frightened, thinking he has wet his bed. This is why it is very important that a boy should be told well in advance of the wet dream experience so that he can be pleased when it happens rather than alarmed. And a boy *should* be pleased; it is a symbol of his developing manhood.

What has actually happened during his dream is that semen has been thrown out of his body during an *orgasm*. This word describes the sense of great pleasure that accompanies the ejaculation of sperm from the penis. First of all the penis becomes hard and erect with extra blood. The reason for this is that the sperm are designed not just to be thrown out of the man's body but to be thrown out in such a way that they have the opportunity of meeting a female egg cell and going on to make a baby. However, as will be seen later when we look at the anatomy of a girl, the sperm has to be deposited inside a woman's body before it can have any chance of meeting an egg cell. But in order for this to happen, the penis must become firm and large enough to go into the female vagina. It can't do this if it's small and relaxed and soft, and this is why there is this system of making it hard and stiffly erect (Fig. 5).

Most boys will know about *erections* (the name given to the hardening of the penis) long before they reach puberty because they will have had them almost as long as they can remember. From earliest babyhood the penis 'rehearses' its ability to be erect from time to time. Most mothers know the way a baby boy's penis becomes erect as soon as the nappy is taken off. All this is perfectly normal and is generally quite pleasurable for a little boy.

However, when it happens at puberty it becomes

more than just a bit pleasurable, and may sometimes even get a little bit uncomfortable. It is usually at this stage that a boy discovers that if he rubs his penis rhythmically while thinking sexy thoughts, he can give himself an orgasm and make semen come out. This is called *masturbation* and is a very enjoyable experience. Over the years an enormous amount of rubbish has been talked about masturbation. Perhaps because it is something that is enjoyable it has made people say that it was bad, that it was dangerous, that it caused madness or blindness or grew hair on the palms of the hands and all sorts of similar nonsense. *None of this is true.*

Virtually all boys masturbate at some time or another, generally around the age of puberty but

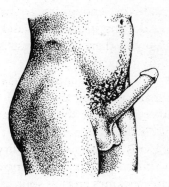

Fig. 5. The penis must fill with blood and become firm and erect before intercourse. The angle of the erection is about the same as the angle of the vagina.

sometimes earlier. In a way it's a rehearsal for the time in the future when as a man, he will make real love with a real woman. In the meantime, there is no harm whatsoever in a boy masturbating from time to time as long as it doesn't become such an obsession with him that he's hardly ever doing anything else. For the vast majority of people the only harmful effects of masturbation are those that come from the way the boy feels about it. If he's made to feel ashamed or guilty, it will be his shame and his guilt that makes him feel bad, not the actual masturbation.

From the age of puberty onwards, a boy will have nocturnal emissions perhaps two or three times in a week, though this varies enormously from individual to individual. It will also depend on how much he masturbates. Very often when a boy first discovers the pleasures of masturbation he may have an orgasm every day or more often. It must be said again that he can't do himself any physical harm by doing this because his testicles are perfectly capable of creating more sperm. About 250 million sperm are ejected every time a boy has an orgasm, even though only one would ever be needed to fertilise a female egg. Nature always has been excessively generous with her provision for creating the next generation!

With this understanding of the way a boy's body is built and how it works during puberty, we can go on to look at what happens to girls.

What Happens To Girls

The age of puberty in girls varies just as it does in boys but on the whole tends to occur at a younger age. This is why so many girls seem to be so much more advanced than boys of the same age, and in mixed sex schools the boys can be made to feel very young and foolish because of the way girls suddenly start to outstrip them in growth, development and apparent sophistication. It's of little comfort to tell these boys that in a few years they will not only catch up with the girls but outstrip them as far as size is concerned, but it is true, all the same.

The big difference in puberty as it happens to girls is that there is a very definite event which pinpoints the passage of the individual from the childhood to adulthood, which is not the case in boys. In girls, the first *period* is considered to be the exact moment of 'growing up'. But in fact this is not the point at which puberty begins.

Just as in boys, puberty in girls is heralded by a definite growth spurt. Also, some girls may become a good deal plumper, while others may become thin, though on the whole girls don't develop quite such a bony, gangly look as do boys. At about the same time the early signs of classic femininity appear to match the masculine ones that appear in boys. Girls start to lay down fat on their bodies in a more obviously feminine way; they develop pads of fat over the hips and the bottom and thighs which has the effect of making the waist look a good deal narrower. At the same time, fat is laid down across the shoulders, the upper arms and most noticeably of all around the nipples on the front of the chest. The breasts begin to grow, and this too has a very marked effect on the waist, and creates the familiar curvy female shape.

At the same time as the development of breasts and a shapelier form, hair begins to grow on the girl's body just as it does on the boy's. The average pattern of hair growth for girls is under the arms and in an inverted triangle over the pad of fat between the groins. The classic male pubic hair growth is diamond shaped with the hair curving back to meet in an apex at the navel. But having said that these are the average patterns, it must be repeated that an enormous number of people do not fit into the so-called average. There are plenty of girls who grow hair across the chest, between the breasts or around the nipples and across the belly. Some develop hair on the arms and legs, and some also in the beard area of the face. Because of the tendency in our society to like defining stereotypes — patterns of what men and women are supposed to look like – girls who develop these sorts of hairiness may become very distressed even though for them it is an inherited tendency and in no way any sign of an abnormality. If a girl is worried about the way her body hair is growing it's always worth discussing the matter with the family doctor. If it is an inherited tendency he might be able to reassure her but also he can make investigations to check that her hormone balance is as it should be.

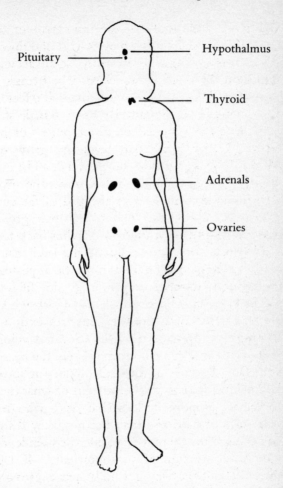

Pituitary

Hypothalmus

Thyroid

Adrenals

Ovaries

Fig. 6. The endocrine glands control the body's growth and development.

While all these obvious changes are taking place on the surface of the girl's body, other changes are happening inside. The uterus is beginning to develop as are the structures associated with it, together with the surface sex organs. And this is a good point at which to stop and look at precisely what sort of sex organs a girl has.

Running from the base of the spine at the back around the body to meet at the front just above the groins there is a girdle of bone called the pelvis. It can be quite easily felt if the hands are put on the hips and the fingers are run forwards and downwards along the edge of the bony crest. The pelvis is of course present in both men and women, but in women is generally rather broader than it is in men.

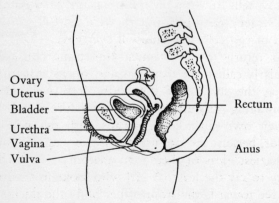

Ovary
Uterus
Bladder
Urethra
Vagina
Vulva
Rectum
Anus

Fig. 7. A side view of a woman's external and internal sex organs.

Tucked behind the pelvis in front, deep inside the body, lie the internal sex organs (Fig. 7.); first, the *uterus* — a hollow, thick muscle-walled organ, with a special very remarkable lining that renews itself every month. At the bottom end of the uterus is a 'neck', properly called the *cervix*, which points downwards into the *vagina*. This is the passageway that leads to the surface of the body. In each of the top corners of the uterus there is a *fallopian tube*. These are the highways along which sperm will have to travel to reach the egg cell, properly called an *ovum*, before a baby can be created. There are two *ovaries* which produce these egg cells and they lie close to the sides of the uterus on each side, under the protective umbrella which is at the end of each of the fallopian tubes. Each ovary contains thousands and thousands of tiny cells all of which are capable of becoming eggs. Every baby girl is born with the full complement of egg cells that she will ever have.

To return to the vagina; this important tube, popularly called 'the front passage' opens at its other end at the surface of the body. It is well worth encouraging girls at puberty — or before — to look at their own surface sex organs with the aid of a mirror, because far too many girls grow up with only the haziest ideas of their own anatomy — which is a pity to say the least. A girl who looks in a mirror will see towards the front of her body the thick soft pad of fat which covers the bony pelvis and on which the curly pubic hair grows; then, running further back from this pad, she will see two thick skin and hair covered outer 'lips'. Lying within them there are two wrinkled, pink mucous membrane covered inner 'lips'(*membrane* is the name of the tissue that lines all body openings, for example the mouth and the nose, as well as the sex organs.) It is important to know that these inner lips also grow at the time of puberty and may grow very unevenly. Sometimes both are rather large and stick out beyond the outer lips, or sometimes just one becomes extra long and sticks out and sometimes both of them may remain short. The variation is as great as it is with faces. Every one of these differences is absolutely normal, and every girl should know this because too many become very agitated when the inner lip growth starts, even suspecting that they are growing a penis and changing sex.

At the point where the two inner lips meet, towards the front of the body, there is a tiny knob of very sensitive tissue indeed. This is called the *clitoris*. This is a bit like a boy's penis because it too, is made of erectile tissue; it becomes stiff and more prominent as a result of sexual excitement. Most girls find out around the age of puberty that rubbing the clitoris gives them a very nice feeling, and that if the rubbing continues for a while, they get a strong uprush of very pleasant feeling. This is called an orgasm, just as in boys, though girls don't have any semen to leave their body. However, they may find that they become very moist when they masturbate,

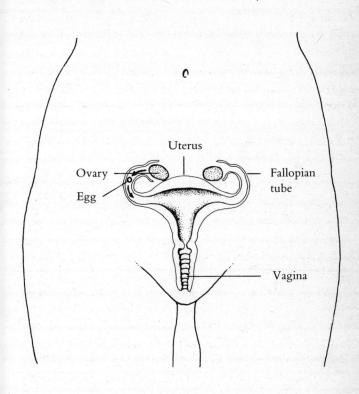

Fig. 8. The uterus, tubes, ovaries and vagina.

but this is normal and nothing to worry about. The moisture is necessary for sexual intercourse (see page 58). Once again, girls need reassuring that there is no harm in masturbating. It's a perfectly natural part of growing up.

Below the clitoris is a tiny hole called the *urethra*. Not everyone is able to see this hole because it is tucked so well inside the pink membrane. It is the opening from the bladder. Girls, unlike boys, have two separate openings — one to deal with urine and the other to deal with reproduction, and the vagina is the one that deals with reproduction. It opens just below the little urethra and in a very young girl is partly covered by a piece of membrane called the *hymen* (popularly known as the *maidenhead*). Further back still the outer lips thin out to meet in a skin covered area called the *perineum*. Right at the back is the opening called the *anus*. All the surface sex organs together are called the *vulva*. It will be a lot easier to understand all this if you look at Figure 7.

All this works in girls in much the same way as in boys — that is to say, it is the endocrine system that is involved.

The hypothalamus triggers the pituitary to send out one of its many hormones to the ovaries.

The ovary responds by beginning to ripen one of its tiny cells into an egg and at the same time produces a hormone which it sends to the uterus.

This hormone when it arrives at the uterus informs it that an egg cell is about to be produced and that it is possible that there will be a baby to develop.

The uterus then begins to prepare a baby-welcoming lining, layer by layer. This lining is thick, soft and well supplied with blood, for it is blood that carries food and oxygen supplies all round the body.

Meanwhile, the pituitary sends out another hormone in a great surge, and this tells the ovary to release the most ripe of its egg cells.

The little balloon on the surface of the ovary in which the egg cell was ripening immediately bursts out and the egg comes out.

This has the effect of persuading the ovary to produce another hormone from the site of the burst balloon, and this goes to the uterus with the urgent message that the egg cell has been produced and there may soon be a baby.

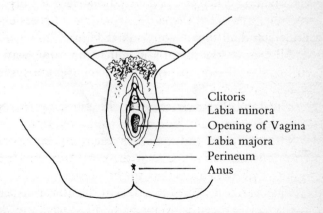

Fig. 9. The vulva — the surface sex organs.

The uterus immediately thickens the lining even more, bringing in extra blood supplies.

At the same time, some of the hormone goes to the breasts warning *them* that in the near future there may be a baby and that they will have to start preparing for their later job of making milk for it. The milk making cells inside the breasts at once start to become active.

All this is felt by the individual girl in different ways. Some girls become very aware of tenseness and tenderness of the breasts and find their breasts may become noticeably larger. There may also be a sense of fullness in the belly and a general 'plumping up'. This is because the hormone that is instructing the uterus and the breasts also has the effect of building up water supplies in all the cells of the body.

The newly shed ripe egg now moves into the fallopian tube, being beckoned in by the waving fingers at the end of the tube (see Fig. 8.) and starts its journey along the tube towards the waiting uterus. It is at this stage that it's possible for fertilisation to occur if a man puts sperm at the opening to the uterus. Later (on pages 59, 60 and 61) you will see exactly what does happen if fertilisation does take place. But now let's consider what happens if it doesn't.

The egg reaches the uterus, taking about ten days to make the journey from the ovary.

Once it gets there it is no longer any use for baby-making and the hormone that has been coming from the ovary falters.

The messages change, and the pituitary moves in once more, instructing the ovary to start egg ripening all over again in the hope that next month there will be fertilising sperm available.

The unwanted lining in the uterus, now overripe and stale, starts to crumble.

The extra fluid and blood brought in, in the hope of a baby, is now no longer needed and the whole lot, lining, blood, elderly egg and all, is thrown right out of the uterus so that the whole process can start all over again.

It is this process that is *menstruation* — popularly called a *period*. For a few days blood seeps away from the uterus out of the vagina, through the gap in the hymen to the surface of the body. While all this is going on, the breasts subside, disappointed, from their ready-to-make-milk state, and settle down to wait for the message to alert them again next month. The whole process from egg-shedding (called *ovulation*) takes about twenty-eight days, which is why periods are said to be monthly ones. On pages 75-80 there will be information on coping with some of the problems of periods, such as choosing the right sanitary protection, aspects of hygiene and so on.

3   Men and Women Together

All the differences between adult men and women exist for one reason only; to make it possible for new human beings to be made. A woman has broader hips than a man because she has to have extra space inside her where babies can grow. A woman has larger breasts than a man because she has to make milk to feed babies. With an understanding of these differences, it is now possible to see how a man and woman together make a baby.

If you look back again at what happens to girls' bodies when they have periods, you will remember that each month an egg cell is produced in the hope that a man's sperm will come along to meet it. Each cell can be *fertilised* — the proper name for a meeting of male and female cells — only for two or three days after it has left the ovary, and while it is travelling along the fallopian tube on its way to the uterus. How can a sperm cell reach that egg?

The way this is made possible is called *sexual intercourse*.

What happens is this. A couple lie close together, sharing kisses, cuddles and caresses, stroking each other. This has the effect of stimulating their sexual feelings. When a man gets sexual feelings, he develops an erection (as described on page 42). When a woman does, she finds that a slippery liquid starts to come from her vagina, making her vulva smooth and extra moist. Both these things happen to make it possible for the man to put his penis inside the vagina; if the penis were not stiff it could not enter the vagina, which is a *soft* tube, remember (a bit like an empty tube of toothpaste) and if the vagina were dry it would not be possible for the penis to move easily inside it, which is necessary, for it is movement that stimulates semen to leave the penis.

To put his penis into the vagina, it is obviously necessary for the man and woman to be very close, and there are several ways in which this is possible. The one that is best known is the face to face; the woman lies on her back with her knees bent and spread apart, so that the man can lie above her. However, he may approach her while they are lying side by side, or she can lie above him. There are no rules about this.

The man now moves his body rhythmically, so that his penis moves to and fro inside the woman, and she too moves rhythmically to help the vagina and penis to make comfortable and complete contact.

This stage of moving lasts a short while — sometimes only a matter of a minute or so, though often much longer — and it is completed when both the man and woman experience an orgasm (the uprush of pleasant feeling already described on pages 42 and 50).

One thing must be said here. Orgasms vary very much indeed. Sometimes, for both men and women, it is a very wonderful experience, but at others it is little more than a sort of sneeze feeling which affects the sex organs instead of the nose. Sometimes a woman won't experience an orgasm at all when she and her man make love, perhaps because she is tired, or worried, or upset in some way. But whether she does or not, she can still become pregnant. However, a man must have an orgasm if he is to succeed in making a baby, for unless he does, the semen won't leave his body. It is *occasionally* possible for a man to make a baby without a complete orgasm if his penis is inside the vagina for a little while, because a few sperm may come out by themselves. But generally speaking, the man needs to complete intercourse with an orgasm, if a baby is to be made.

When the semen has been put inside the woman's body, and the woman lies quietly sleeping (most people fell very relaxed and comfortable and sleepy after having intercourse which is why the most popular time for it is at night, in bed) sperm starts to swim up from her vagina, into her cervix,and on its way to the fallopian tubes, each little individual sperm whipping its tadpole–tail to help it along. When the millions of sperm reach the egg cell, they cluster around it, and one — and only one — manages to bury its head in the side of the egg. The woman's egg is much bigger than the man's sperm and there is plenty of room for the sperm to get in. (As a matter of interest, if two sperm meet two separate eggs — which can happen, if the woman's body has unexpectedly ripened two together — the result is twins. They won't be identical; that kind only happens when the combined egg-and-sperm for some unknown reason start to develop into two separate though identical babies) See Figure 10.

The remaining sperm shrivel up and disappear, while the two combined cells now continue the journey to the uterus. All the while they travel, they are busy growing, in a process called *cell division*. The two cells split in half, to make two more cells, and that four split to make eight, and the eight split to make sixteen and so on. By the time the cells reach the uterus there are enough to look like a tiny raspberrry.

This minute object moves towards the wall of the uterus which, you will remember, has been busily preparing a thick warm lining specially for it. It buries itself into the lining, rather like a child diving headfirst into a pile of soft newcut grass, and settles down to grow.

What happens during the next two hundred and eighty days is really almost incredible. Those tiny cells go on growing at a great rate, dividing themselves into different groups, some going to make arms and legs, some making brain and heart, some making nerves and blood — all the parts of a new human being.

As the cells grow and divide and change, some of them develop into a thin bag, full of water, inside which the baby grows, floating safely and happily. However much his mother may move about all he feels is the gentle flow of the water which holds him and absorbs all the unpleasant outside shocks.

Of course the child needs food and air to grow, and he can't get those through his stomach or his lungs, not while he is still developing them. So, some of the cells become a large plate–like organ called the *placenta* which is joined to the baby via a thick rope of twisted blood vessels, called the *umbilical cord*. The placenta attaches itself to the wall of the mother's

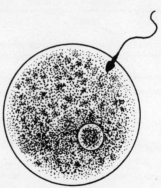

Fig. 10. The tiny sperm buries itself into the large ovum. A new person has started to grow.

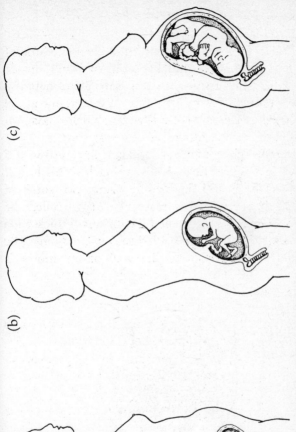

Fig. 10.   (a) 3 months after conception; (b) 6 months after conception; (c) fully grown, 9 months later.

uterus, and collects foodstuffs and oxygen from her blood (she gets the supply from eating and breathing, of course) and passes it along the cord to the baby, so that it goes in to him through the centre of his belly. His waste products pass back along the cord into the mother's blood supply, and she gets rid of them at the same time as she gets rid of her own.

While the baby is growing, the uterus which holds him grows too, so that gradually the mother develops a bump in front as she gets more and more filled up with baby. Then after two hundred and eighty days — forty weeks, or roughly nine calendar months — the baby is full grown. He is ready to leave his mother's body for a separate life of his own (see Figure 11).

Getting in as a very tiny object like a sperm is one thing — quick and very easy. Getting out when you have become a seven pound baby is not so quick. First of all the mother's cervix — the neck of the uterus — has to open wide enough to let the baby out, and then the vagina has to stretch enough to make a passageway for him, and finally the mother has to push with her belly muscles to help her baby on its way. All this is hard work that takes a long time which is why the process of giving birth is called *labour*.

Some people expect labour to be the most dreadful pain in the world, and there is no doubt it can be like that — if the mother is not properly looked after, doesn't understand what is happening in her body, and is allowed to get scared. The stretching of her cervix — which happens in a rhythm of stretch, relax, stretch, relax, called *contractions* can be painful if the muscles are working particularly hard. However, these days women in labour are looked after by experienced doctors and midwives, can have special pain–relieving drugs and can be taught how to relax in such a way they are able to enjoy having their babies. No girl today need ever think that when the time comes for her to have babies that she will suffer dreadfully. She won't — it will be hard work, and sometimes uncomfortable but far from being absolute agony (— some people, though, will tell her otherwise! There is a strange human tendency to make things sound worse than they actually are; films and novels and stories do it all the time for dramatic effect. But no one should ever believe everything they read, or see in a film).

Once the baby has been pushed out of his mother's body after her labour — which usually takes around twelve to fifteen hours, though it can be much shorter or rather longer (and it is only for the last couple of hours or so that the mother is really working hard at pushing out her baby) he has to learn to breathe through his own lungs. The cord that attached him to the placenta is cut (a painless experience for both mother and baby, for it contains no nerve tissue) the placenta is thrown out of the mother's body, and the stump of the cord shrivels away after a few days to leave the familiar navel — the belly button — in the baby's middle.

A newborn baby is often rather messy looking,

because he is covered in a yellowish waxy substance, but this soon washes off. It was there to protect his skin during those long growing weeks in the water inside the bag in which he grew

Virtually as soon as he is born, the baby is ready to feed, and if he is given to his mother, and she holds him to her breast, he will grasp the nipple firmly between his jaws and start pumping away in an attempt to get milk. At first he will get a special substance called *colostrum* which is very yellowish — it looks like extra rich Devonshire cream — and it contains special protective substances which the mother's body makes for him. After about three days the mother's breasts settle down to making true milk. It is very much like the milk made by any other mammal — cows or hares or goats or sheep — but it consists of exactly the right balance of food for the human baby. A cow's milk — which is only ideal for a calf — can be made suitable for a human baby by having some of the fat taken off and extra sugar and water added, but ideally human babies need human milk. In some parts of the world children are breast fed until they are three or even four years old, but in this country, the usual is somewhere between three to nine months. Some mothers can't feed their own babies at all, which is a pity, but their babies do very well being fed prepared cow's milk from a bottle.

It takes the mother's body about six weeks to get back to its before–pregnancy state after a baby is born. Then she is able to make another baby.

4 How Not to Make Babies

If sexual intercourse had only one purpose — to make new babies — then people would only do it when they wanted to have a child. But sexual intercourse is more than a baby–making method. It is the closest two people can get together, the deepest form of physical communication there can be, so for the human species sex and love have come to be very closely entwined. A man and a woman have intercourse because they love each other, as a way of expressing their love for each other, and as a way to make their love grow and strengthen and develop. This is why it is so often called 'making love'.

Some people don't think love matters all that much when it comes to sex. They say it is a very enjoyable human activity — which it is — and they see no reason why it should only be shared by two people who love each other. They argue it is just like eating, really; when you're hungry you eat, and it doesn't matter whether it's something you don't like, like tapioca pudding, or something you love like roast duck or whatever.

Well, people who think this are entitled to their point of view, but is a minority one. Most adults believe — and they base their belief on personal experience — that sex shared by two people as an expression of their love for each other is much more satisfying than sex with someone who just happens along.

Most loving couples find they need to make love quite often. Their feeling for each other builds up and builds up, and needs a chance to express itself. Some couples will make love every night, some two or three times a week, some not so often — but however often it is, one thing is sure. They don't want to make a baby every time. If every woman had as many babies as her body was capable of making, she would have about 30 children. Not only would that be disastrous for her — physically exhausting, to say the least — and misery for her children (for who could possibly give real mothering to a family of thirty?) — it would be dreadful for the world. In a couple of generations or so the planet would be desperately overrun with people. Already many experts think there are far too many people in the world, and that it is vital that tomorrow's parents — today's children — should take it for granted that they have very small families indeed — two at the most.

Fortunately, it is possible for people to make love as often as they wish without at the same time making a baby. The word used to describe starting a baby is *conception*. The word for avoiding making babies is *contraception*.

There are several different ways in which this is possible. If you remember how a baby is made, you will remember it is necessary for a male sperm to meet a female egg. Contraceptive methods are designed to prevent this meeting, and they can do it in several different ways.

Natural Methods

The most obvious is not to make love at all. But this is a very bad method; people who love each other *need* to make love whenever they feel tender and affectionate towards each other. If they can't do this they can become very frustrated and irritable. Anyway, just telling people not to make love is like telling the sun not to rise. It's much too strong a drive to be overcome just like that.

Another so-called 'natural' method which has been used for many centuries is called withdrawal or 'being careful' (it has a Latin name — *coitus interruptus*). It works like this. A couple enjoy intercourse just up to the point when the man feels his orgasm is beginning. Then he very quickly pulls his penis out of the vagina and lets the semen be thrown out of his body outside the woman's vagina. The idea is that this will prevent any sperm getting into the woman's body and reaching an egg cell.

However, this is a very bad method for several reasons. First of all, as we've already seen, it is possible for some sperm to leave the man's penis even before he has an orgasm, so as a method of preventing a pregnancy it's a very inefficient one. Secondly, it is very unnatural in many ways for a man to pull away from his partner at this point in intercourse. All his natural instincts make him want to be as close to her as he possibly can so that he can leave his semen deeply inside her. To force himself to pull away just at this moment is really an insult to his very nature. Similarly, the natural thing for a woman to want at this point of intercourse is to be as close to her partner as possible, and to have him suddenly pull away in this way is very alarming for her. So the method not only spoils love making for the couple—it can't even be guaranteed to prevent a pregnancy.

The third 'natural' method of birth control is one that at present is the only one allowed by the Catholic church. It is called the *rhythm method* and is based on a very careful study of a woman's menstrual cycle. You will remember that the egg cell a woman produces can only be fertilised during the first two or three days after it leaves her ovary and while it is travelling along the fallopian tube to the uterus. If it is possible for a couple to work out exactly when that egg is produced, they can then know on which days it is possible for the egg to be fertilised. They then make sure that they don't make love on those days.

The method sounds very simple, but there is a problem about it. No woman menstruates just like clockwork. Although periods are said to happen once a month, and in fact some women do have their periods every twenty-eight days, most women find there is a considerable variation. Their periods may come every five weeks or every three weeks, and sometimes there may be as much as one or two weeks' difference between every period. So they can't know exactly when their eggs will be produced from the ovary. However, some couples are able to use this method fairly successfully once they have got used to the individual woman's personal cycle.

Barrier Methods

This group of methods means that a physical barrier is put between the meeting of the sperm and the egg cell. This can be done either by the man using a barrier to prevent his sperm getting into his partner's body or the woman can use a barrier to cover the neck of her uterus—the cervix—so that the sperm can't get in.

The barrier that the man uses is a very well known one. It is a fine 'sleeve' of very soft thin rubber and its proper name is *sheath* or *condom*. It is also popularly known as a French letter or as a *Durex* (the last one being the most famous brand available in this country). It is put on the erect penis before intercourse and then when all the sperm come out when the man has his orgasm, they are caught in the sleeve of rubber. Then when intercourse is completed the man can take off the sleeve. This method is used by a great many people, and it is safe if properly used.

The barriers that a woman may use are similar in principle, the cervix being closed off by a device made of soft rubber. Some of these devices are flat and have a spiral ring round their edge. Others are shaped like thimbles and slip right over the cervix. The woman has to put it inside her vagina, fairly high up, well before intercourse. These devices have various names like 'Dutch' cap or cervical cap.

These have to be specially fitted for individual women. It is not usual just to buy them at a chemist's shop as you can buy sheaths.

Destruction of Cells

This group of methods involve destroying one or other of the cells before they can meet and unite. There is no way of destroying female ova once they have been ejected from the ovary, and before they have been fertilised, because they are much too deep inside a woman's body. It is possible, however, to destroy the man's sperm after it has been ejected from his body and before it can swim up inside the woman's body to meet an ovum. This is done with chemicals. If a woman puts into her vagina a special substance such as a foam, a cream, or a paste containing the chemical, when the sperms are ejected from the man they meet the chemical and this destroys them. There are a great many forms available and they can be bought in any chemist's shop.

However, they do have drawbacks. The most important thing is that they are really not very efficient. Nobody has yet found a chemical method that would *completely* destroy all the sperm that are put inside a woman's body. And if a chemical destroys two million but leaves just one healthy one available to swim up into the uterus, then it's still possible for pregnancy to start. Chemicals are very useful if used together with a sheath and cap, and especially helpful in preventing the spread of some sexually transmitted diseases (see page 91).

Non-production of Cells

An even better way of making sure that the two cells can't meet up to make a baby is to stop one or other of them being made at all! This is the most modern method of contraception available and is, of course, the Pill.

Very simply, the Pill works by stopping the woman's ovaries from producing eggs that could be fertilised. There are lots of different types, but basically they all work in the same way. They are made of hormones that a woman has to take every day in the form of a Pill and they definitely interfere with the woman's own hormones in such a way that they stop an egg from being produced from the ovary.

The drawback to the Pill is that it doesn't agree with all women. Some get headaches, feel sick, put on weight or get very tender breasts, and in a very few, rare cases women have been made ill or even died because of it. But it is important to know that these *are* rare; the risk of taking the Pill is less than the risk of being pregnant and having a baby, and everyone knows how safe it is to have a baby these days.

The Pill has to be prescribed for every woman individually by a doctor to make sure that it is suitable for her and that she is not at any risk if she takes it.

It is also possible to arrange matters so that a man doesn't produce any sperm. It is possible in an operation to cut the little tube that carries the newly developed sperm from the man's testicles to his penis. This does not alter his ability to have erections and to have intercourse and to have orgasms; it just makes sure that no live sperm are thrown out of his body.

Quite obviously this method is only useful for men who are quite sure they never again want to father any babies. It is a permanent method and is only used for adult men who have completed their families.

A woman, too, can be *sterilised* — the name for this operation—by having her fallopian tubes blocked in such a way that no egg cells can reach the uterus from the ovary. Once again this is only suitable for women who have already had all the children they want and are quite certain they will never again want any more.

The IUD

This method (the letters are short for Intra-Uterine Device) doesn't work like any of the others. In fact nobody is quite sure how it does work. Briefly, it is a very small plastic covered device which is put inside the woman's uterus by a doctor. Experts think it probably works by preventing a fertilised ovum from embedding itself into the lining of the uterus so that it can grow into a baby. Once it is put into the uterus a woman can forget all about it. It can remain there for many years, simply needing to be checked by the doctor every year. It's quite a good method but there have been some failures with it because quite a number of women are unable to hold on to the device, and also some women have developed infections because of it.

Old Wives' Tales

A lot of very strange ideas go around about how to prevent birth. Some women think they can prevent themselves from getting pregnant if they pee — pass urine — immediately after having intercourse. But this obviously isn't true, because if you look again at Figure 7, page 48 you will see that the opening to the bladder is quite separate from the vagina. So no amount of passing of water will wash away any sperm.

There is also a very strange idea that intercourse that is carried out in certain positions won't result in a pregnancy. Some young people, for example, have been told that intercourse is safe if experienced while standing up. But this is definitely not true. It is, of course, obvious that some of the semen will come out of the woman's body by the force of gravity if she is standing up when she has intercourse, but it only takes one, remember, to get into the uterus to make a baby and it is always possible for one to do just that.

This is a very brief account of some of the methods of birth control that are available. People who need to know more about it can get individual help at Family Planning Association Clinics (see p. 100).

5 Living With Sex

Since puberty is so complex a phase of life, and takes so long — it is several years before it can be said that the change from childhood to adulthood is complete — it is inevitable that there will be some problems associated with it. Some are specific to girls, some to boys, and some to both sexes.

Girls' Problems

Obviously, coping with a three to six-day flow of blood from the vagina every four or five weeks can be a nuisance. A girl needs to come to practical terms with the business of menstrual hygiene as early as she can for the sooner she is able to take it all in her stride the happier she will be.

First of all she needs to understand that menstruation is normal, is not in any way a disease (the old fashioned trick of describing have a period as 'being unwell' is something no modern parent ought to go along with!) and is nothing to be afraid of. It's as

normal as eating or drinking or going to the lavatory.
A nuisance, undeniably, but it needn't be more than
that.

Some girls do suffer from pains, headaches,
sickness and general distress when they have their
periods. This may be due to unexpressed fear of what
is happening; a girl who hasn't had a clear explanation
of normal periods is obviously going to be alarmed
by them, so it's important for every girl to be helped
by being given clear and accurate facts about what
is happening to her body. But by no means all girls
suffering from such nasty periods are showing a
psychological response (as once used to be said) for
they may, in these early months of adult life, have
a hormone imbalance. It is possible for a doctor to
give hormone treatment that will give rapid relief of
symptoms, so any girl suffering in this way should
see a doctor at once.

In general terms, a girl who has plenty of rest, ex-
ercise, a well balanced diet that prevents constipation
(including lots of fresh green vegetables, raw fruit,
wholemeal bread, plenty of fluids and a minimum
of fattening greasy foods) will have no trouble with
periods.

Coping with the flow is something that needs to
be sorted out early. Some girls in the early months
have a very heavy flow indeed, and need to take
special care to avoid embarrassing leaks. For them,
soft disposable surface pads — sanitary towels —
worn with a pair of protective briefs (the 'Nikini' type

are good) is best. Later on when the period pattern and degree of flow has been established, there is no reason why the girl shouldn't use tampons — pledgets of compressed cotton which are inserted inside the vagina to catch the flow there. These are very comfortable and perfectly safe to use, though if the flow is very heavy, they may be somewhat inadequate. There is no truth in the idea that single girls can't use tampons, any more than there is in the idea that their use 'takes away virginity'. A virgin is a girl who has not experienced sexual intercourse. The fact that she has used a small object like a tampon inside her vagina doesn't alter that status at all.

Some girls have a little difficulty in using a tampon because the hymen — the flap of membrane over the vagina — has too small a gap in it to allow the tampon in. This is fairly rare, and generally gentle perseverance with the tampons will make it possible for the girl to use them comfortably in time. It is a very good thing for a girl to learn to handle her own body by using tampons, for it will make sure she is less nervous and anxious about herself when she is an adult and ready for a full sexual relationship. And there are other benefits of tampons: because the discharged blood does not come into contact with the air there is no unpleasant odour; they are easy to dispose of and fresh supplies are easy to carry; and they cause no awkward bumps to show under tight skirts or trousers. If difficulty with using tampons persists, however, it is well worth arranging to see a doctor to make sure that the hymen is not in need of gentle stretching. If the family doctor can't be approached (some girls are too shy to approach him — unnecessarily, of course, but that's the way people are) help can be had with this matter at a Family Planning Association Clinic (see p. 100).

As long as a girl is taught the importance of sufficiently frequent changing of towel and tampon and the importance of careful washing — and, of course, it is absolute rubbish that a girl shouldn't bath or wash her hair during a period — she should have no problems in coping with this normal adult function. And she *won't* need the expensive vaginal "deodorants" that are so widely advertised. As long as she washes regularly, that's enough. There is a normal natural body smell that does not need masking in any way, and is certainly nothing to worry about.

Another problem of periods for many girls is the condition known as *pre menstrual tension*. The sufferer finds that in the week or so before her period she becomes rather headachy, moody and irritable, may get spotty on the face and back, have lank hard-to-manage hair, and may get noticeably plumper and have sore breasts. This happens because the body builds up an extra fluid supply in the hope of a pregnancy. When the period starts the extra fluid is thrown out as extra urine, and the girl immediately feels much better.

If a girl notices she is particularly moody, depressed and tearful at this time, and has some of these other symptoms, she should talk to her doctor. A great deal can be done to help with this problem nowadays.

Many girls worry during these growing years because of their breast development — or lack of it. One very important piece of reassurance that needs to be given to girls is that breast growth is *not* always even. Some girls are very disconcerted when they find that one breast grows before the other, or if they discover one is markedly larger than the other. Most girls in fact find this unevenness levels off later on and that anyway the variation in what is normal in breast size, shape and development is very wide indeed. Because the breasts are so obvious and such a well-known symbol of femininity a great many girls become very distressed if theirs don't fit into an image of what the girl herself thinks breasts ought to look like — an image which is set by pictures of nudes in magazines. Girls need to be reassured that the models they see in magazines are far from being typical of all women, that many of them have their breasts stuck up with sellotape to make them look more tilted than they really are, and that there is a good deal of clever use of makeup. It is important to reassure a developing girl of this because too many are made to feel somehow less feminine and less attractive than they really are because of this false idea that they have been given.

The same is true of nipple development. Some girls have smooth nipples, some have inverted ones. Some find their nipples are very sensitive to cold (they are made of erectile tissue and become wrinkled and firm when exposed to cold, or when the girl is sexually excited) others find they are less so. They are all normal. It is also worth repeating the point that the distribution of body hair can vary enormously from girl to girl. All these variations are *normal*.

Vaginal Discharge

It is normal for a healthy adult woman's vagina to produce a certain amount of mucus. This is often rather heavier just before a period. It also increases as a response to sexual excitement.

As long as the discharge is clear, non-smelly and dries to a whitish patch on clothes, no need to worry. If it becomes discoloured or smelly, however, a doctor's help will be needed; there may be the common and annoying infection called *thrush*. This is easy to treat, however, so no girl need ever be afraid of seeing her doctor about it.

Boys' Problems

Although boys are blessedly free of the discomforts and nuisance aspects) of menstruation, it should never be thought that they have no problems at all. They have their own, and it may be more difficult for them to find the support and help they need, simply because they don't have the obvious sign of developing adulthood that girls enjoy. People who are ready to make allowances for a girl because 'it's her periods' will be far less willing to make them for boys — yet they do have similar difficulties, especially when it comes to mood swings.

There will be times when the boy going through this stage of his life will feel extremely aggressive either towards his friends or to his parents, while at others he will be extremely emotional and warm, even tearful and clinging; there will be times when he is full of energy and so active and busy that he exhausts everyone around him, while at others he seems sunk in apathy and lethargy, totally uninterested in anything at all. He may be at the top of his emotional tree, full of happiness and excitement at one moment and almost immediately afterwards swing to a deep dejected sulk.

All this is profoundly irritating for the adults — parents and teachers — with whom the boy has to be involved but a great deal more distressing for the boy himself. He is as alarmed and upset by the way he reacts to the world around him as anyone else.

Most experienced teachers and youth workers are well aware of this and are able to be relaxed and uncritical of a boy's occasional odd behaviour and find that he returns to his usual good humour very quickly. It may not be as easy for parents to be as understanding and accepting as this, however, especially with the first boy in the family, but if they can see this behaviour as very much a part of the growing up stage they will be less likely to make life difficult for themselves.

For example, it is often during the stage of puberty that a boy shows the first signs of the necessary adolescent rebellion. Necessary, because without it he would never escape from the nursery atmosphere of childhood to make a life for himself as a man. In its earlier stages this affirmation of individuality is very irritating. It *is* annoying when a boy refuses to wash, grows his hair into a style which you as an adult find displeasing, is bad-tempered, slams doors and so on. But if this can be seen for what it is — an attempt to come to grips with the difficulties of being an adult — parents will be less likely to overreact and so create more trouble than is necessary. Making a great deal of fuss over fairly unimportant things, such as the length of a boy's hair, or the style of his clothes, is a very sure way to create an atmosphere of hostility in the home that can go on long after puberty has passed and the boy has become a civilised adult.

Something else that worries parents at puberty is another very common emotional change — intense group identification. A boy who is beginning to turn his back on the closeness of his family unit has to seek another group outside the family, and his usual choice is among boys of his own age. The resulting 'gang phenomenon' is one of the oldest known to mankind.

Right from the beginning of human times boys going through puberty have shown very clearly indeed their need to belong to a group, and they function much more happily when they're accepted members of the group to which they want to belong. This is fine if the group they choose is one that is socially acceptable. The boy who wants to become the star of a rugger team or who wants to get involved with a local youth club is obviously going to do very well. But if he gets involved with an anti-social group, then the situation is rather different. Even the most carefully brought up of boys, with a strong sense of what is right and wrong, can be swept into law-breaking behaviour if he happens to select for himself a group that engages in these sorts of activities.

Wise parents are always forewarned about this possibility; if they can make sure that in the pre-pubertal years their son is given the opportunity to choose his friends from among the sort of young people whose later ganging will not lead them into hooliganism or other forms of law-breaking, it will help a great deal. Certainly the worst thing to do if a boy does get involved with such a gang is to display distrust, dislike or anger about the gang; this will only increase his loyalty to the gang because it immediately provides him with an ideal area in which to be rebellious. Much cleverer a way to deal with this sort of reaction during the pubertal and post-pubertal years it to hold open house for the gang. If a group of boys, however surly and anti-adult they may seem to be, can be helped to feel that the home of one of their members is a place where they are welcome and treated as worthwhile individuals in their own right, it is a lot easier to bring them into some sort of area of activity that is less dangerous to themselves and to their society. This is a technique that has been used by a great many youth workers, who deliberately invite local troublemakers into a club and ask them to do a job of work — such as decorating or building — to give them the sense of belonging to a worthwhile group.

It is also worth knowing that during this time of development a great many boys develop a great need for privacy. The boy who has hitherto been perfectly happy to share a room with his brother and who has been quite content to join in the rough and tumble of ordinary family life takes to locking himself in his room on his own listening to his favourite records and generally brooding.

This, too, is normal behaviour and if treated with respect — that is, if the boy is allowed his periods of uninterrupted privacy — will enrich his life rather than make him solitary. It's only when parents nag at the boy who wants to be left alone sometimes that the boy withdraws further and further into his own solitariness.

Everyone's Problems

One of the problems of puberty that causes most distress is the skin condition called *acne*. This is a skin condition which affects about eighty per cent of the adolescent population, and although it often begins in the early teens it is not unusual for it to begin as early as the age of ten. Certainly it does not happen before.

It appears on the face, the back, and the chest, and there are several types of spots: blackheads, raised red spots and yellow-headed infected spots.

The cause is probably hormonal, though it is thought that there may also be an inherited tendency (certainly having relations who have suffered from acne makes it more likely that a particular child will). People who have acne produce more grease on their skins than other people. The skin is equipped with special glands which produce a substance called *sebum*, which is meant to lubricate the skin. People who have acne find that these *sebaceous glands* become blocked with an excess of sebum, and it is this that causes the raised spots and the blackheads. If these become infected — which they often do — the result is the familiar pus-filled spots. These often heal to leave the well-known pitted scar.

Many cases of acne improve by themselves at around the age of eighteen, though this cannot be guaranteed. And even after the condition has cleared up the face may be left scarred.

Treatment should always be sought from a doctor. Too many young skins have been made much worse than they need because of attempts at self-treatment.

Generally recommended is twice daily washing of the infected areas with water as hot as can be borne and plenty of soap. The heat opens the affected

pores and the soap washes away the excess sebum.
In addition to this, the skin should be cleaned
regularly with a special detergent, recommended by
the doctor.

Blackheads should be removed but *never* by
squeezing with the fingers. This can lead to infection
and greater scarring. Blackheads are best removed
with a small instrument called a *comedone extractor*,
which can be bought at a chemist's shop for a few
pence.

Because there have been theories about the effect of
certain foods on the production of skin sebum, some
doctors will recommend that the adolescent should
not eat fried foods and should cut out sweets and
various carbohydrate foods. Others do not believe
that the diet has any effect at all.

Some doctors will give antibiotics to control
infection, while others will recommend ultra-violet
ray treatment. It has been noticed that some patients
have much less trouble with their acne when the skin
is exposed to natural sunlight.

Some doctors may recommend a hormone treatment, while others believe that a course of vitamins
A and D will help.

Surface treatment can be given in the form of
special creams which will peel off the upper layers
of the skin and in many cases this is helpful. In very
severe cases surgical treatment in which the skin
is actually planed by a plastic surgeon to remove
permanent scars may be useful.

Crushes

It is all too easy for adults to laugh at the pangs of young love, but it is really cruel — and extraordinarily forgetful — to do so. When you stop to think that every adult was once an adolescent and suffered exactly the same miseries as today's adolescents, it really is incredible that so many of them have been able to forget what it felt like, and offer teasing instead of sympathy to their own adolescents.

Falling wildly in love with some unattainable person is a characteristic of being young. It's a form of rehearsal for the coming time when the young person will fall in love properly. So it's *necessary* for development.

Many young people choose to fall in love with a pop star, or a sports hero or heroine. This is natural, and though very painful for the person experiencing it, nothing to get agitated about. Indeed, it can be a very growing sort of experience; getting a crush on a famous actor and going to see everything he ever does can have the effect of introducing a young person to the pleasures of the theatre, to the work of Shakespeare and Shaw and other great literary figures in a very special and worthwhile way. Similarly, falling head over ears for a singer can be a way of getting a young person really interested in music.

Sensible parents never jeer or mock at a teenage crush of this sort. Not only do they fail to alter the child's feelings (if that is what they want to do) but they make the child feel misunderstood and unable to seek support and help from the people most suited to give it to them — their own parents. How could a young man talk sensibly about his feelings to someone who mocks him?

When a youngster falls in love with an available person for the first time, say the girl or boy next door, once again their feelings should be treated with respect. There will be many more such fallings in love to come, as every adult knows, but to the young person him or herself at the time this is the only one that matters, and it should never be mocked at. It is the cruellest and most thoughtless thing to do, and any adult tempted to tease a twelve or thirteen year old about his or her love should stop and think how they would feel if someone started mocking them for their love for their partner. They would be hurt just as bitterly.

When it comes to falling in love with a person of the same sex, many young people get very agitated. There is no need for this alarm; it is very natural and normal for there to be a phase of feeling something between love and hero-worship for a person of your own sex. In the days when most children went to one sex schools everyone knew about it, but hardly anyone talked about it. Today when young people go to co-educational schools, they are often pressured by advertising and popular entertainment to fall in love with the opposite sex, and then are startled to find that later on they fall in love with their own. But this doesn't mean that they are homosexual; simply that they are using the adored person as a model for themselves. The time will come when the child will grow out of his or her need for such a model, and will turn to the opposite sex.

Homosexuality

Having mentioned the commonness of crushes upon people of the same sex in adolescence this is a good point to look at the state of homosexuality.

A homosexual is in simple terms a person, either man or woman, who finds it impossible to feel sexual love for people of the opposite sex. They find that sexual love is only inspired by people of their own sex. The word used to describe men who react like this is simply *homosexual*; for women it is *lesbian*.

Some hard facts: about ten per cent of all people are estimated to be totally homosexual, that is responding only to the same sex. About ten per cent of people are probably totally heterosexual, that is responding only to the opposite sex. The rest of us — eighty per cent — are along a line between the two. Most people have a streak, as it were, of oppositeness in them. Most women have women friends to whom they are very close; most men too have close male friends. Yet no one is surprised by this, or calls it homosexuality. Yet in a way, such friendships are an expression of this mixture of feminine and masculine in both sexes. A totally masculine man is as unimaginable as is a totally feminine woman. Because so few people realise that there is this natural two-sidedness to all of us, all sorts of stupid tales are told about homosexuals. They are said to be wicked, and only interested in seducing young people. This is no more true than that all heterosexual people are interested in seducing the very young. There are, of course, some people who are sexually disturbed, and can only find their sexual pleasure in approaching children, and children of both sexes, of course, need to be warned about the sort of person who approaches them in the street, or tries to lure them away; but it would be very wrong to say that only one group did this. It can be both heterosexuals and homosexuals.

It is also not true that certain occupations are more homosexual than others. There are just as many homosexual lorry drivers as there are homosexual hairdressers; just as many heterosexual ballet dancers as there are heterosexual plumbers.

Nor is it true that certain physical types are more likely to be homosexual. Small delicately built men can be just as heterosexual as great big rugby playing giants; big strong women are just as feminine as tiny bird-boned types.

And it is, above all, sheer nonsense to suggest that an interest in certain subjects labels a person as homosexual. Too many boys have been made to feel ashamed and afraid because they are interested in art, in design, in classical music or cooking or fashion (and there is no reason why a boy shouldn't be!)

just as too many girls have been whispered about at school because they liked football matches, fast cars and the taste of beer. They too are entitled to have any interests they fancy having.

So anyone who labels a homosexual as 'queer' and sneers at them, or laughs at them, is displaying a very sad lack of understanding of basic human nature. Homosexuals are not any more wicked or queer than anyone else. They may be somewhat different in their sexual needs, but that doesn't make them better or worse than anyone else. Just *different*.

Venereal Diseases

Properly called the sexually transmitted diseases, these illnesses present a very big problem to society today. Spread by sexual intercourse, some of them in particular are very dangerous illnesses and should never be treated lightly. Before going on to describe the diseases in some detail, one thing must be said here. It is *promiscuous* sex that spreads these illnesses. A loving couple, who make love only with each other, never with anyone else, do not get the infections. People who sleep around, however, going from partner to partner without caring at all who the people they go with have been with before, are at great risk of sooner or later being a contact of the pool of disease that is carried by those people who are promiscuous.

It is also important to know that these diseases are nothing to do with dirt. You can bathe every day, wash three times a day, but if you have promiscuous sex then you are at risk. If you never wash, are as dirty as an unscrubbed slaughter house but are not promiscuous then you won't get any venereal disease (you may catch other diseases — probably will! — but they won't be the venereal ones). VD *cannot* be caught from public lavatories, or from seats in public transport, or from standing in a crowd next to a sufferer. It is promiscuous sex that is the spreader.

The diseases which cause the most concern to specialists in this field are *AIDS, syphilis, gonorrhoea, chlamydia,* and *genital warts,* which may cause cancer of the cervix in women, and this account will show you exactly why.

AIDS

This is a disease about which there has been a lot of talk but sadly few facts.

It is caused by a virus called human immuno-deficiency virus, HIV for short. There are several forms of this virus, and they have very dangerous effects. They damage the body's ability to fight off infections of all sorts, and that means that a person with HIV may be destroyed by a germ that does no harm at all to people who have not been so damaged.

If a person collects the virus, which is carried in body fluids, especially blood and semen, he or she has that virus for life. But — and this is important — that person may seem perfectly healthy, but will still be able to pass on the virus. Not all the people who have the virus go on to develop the full blown disease called *AIDS* (which stands for acquired immune deficiency syndrome) and at present there is no way of knowing how many of the people who do collect the virus will go on to get the disease.

The symptoms vary according to the part of the body affected (and this can be very variable) and include forms of pneumonia, gut infections and skin diseases.

At present there is no cure for AIDS infections — but it is a very preventable illness. The virus is a fragile one and hard to catch, so sensible sexual behaviour will always protect.

That means people should remember two rules; never share sex with a stranger, who might have collected the virus from a previous sexual experience. Only ever make love with someone you know and trust, and ideally love, and who loves you. Then you can feel more sure that you are safe.

But if you can't be sure of your sexual partner, always use a condom, together with a chemical (see contraception information) because the condom prevents the passage of the virus, and the chemical kills it.

If young people grow up remembering these two firm guidelines — and the first is really the most important — they need not be frightened of AIDS. Nor need they be afraid of the unfortunate people who have it already.

And, by the way, AIDS is not a disease suffered only by homosexual men. It can be and is a danger to everyone.

Syphilis

This disease has three stages — a primary, a secondary and a tertiary. It is essential that treatment be started early if the disease is to be controlled.

The first sign is a sore on the sex organs, a hard sore which bleeds easily. This sore usually heals without treatment in a few weeks, and this is one of the dangers — the sufferer may think all is well, but in fact is is *not* because the disease then progresses to the secondary stage.

This stage, which occurs a few weeks after the appearance of the first sore, *lasts up to two years*. The symptoms are these:

Rashes, which appear evenly on both sides of the body, are ham-coloured and never itch.

General swelling of the glands in the neck, under the arms, in the groins, and in the abdomen.

Mouth sores — thin narrow white ulcers. Because of the way they look they are called 'snail track' ulcers. The tongue may be red, inflamed and cracked.

The hair may fall out, leading to patchy or complete baldness — in either sex.

Anaemia — a shortage of iron in the blood, which causes tiredness, breathlessness and general feelings of illness.

Sometimes fever and severe headache may occur.

In some cases, there may be meningitis or cerebral thrombosis, conditions which can be fatal.

If no treatment is given during this stage, the disease progresses to the tertiary stage, which causes permanent damage. The tertiary stage may start as early as two years after the appearance of the primary sore, or as late as fifteen years after. The symptoms include:

Deep ulcers, often on the legs, which will not heal.

Inflammation of the bones and joints which causes severe pain, especially at night — commonest in the legs and arms.

Heart damage and damage to blood vessels, especially the main artery called the aorta — which can eventually be fatal.

Nerve damage, leading to paralysis and incurable insanity.

Severe ulcers of the mouth, throat and tongue, leading to destruction of the bones of the face and nose, and permanent damage to the palate, which gives rise to great speech difficulties.

Clearly this is a horrible disease, and what is worse, it can affect not only the sufferer, but unborn children. Children of syphilitic mothers may be stillborn, or very weak and wasted. If they develop at all, they show stunted physical growth and mental handicap.

During the first two stages, the disease is highly infectious, so this is another reason why treatment is essential from the very beginning.

In this country, treatment can be obtained rapidly and confidentially at special venereal disease clinics which are held at most hospitals. Addresses of clinics can be obtained from the local post office or Town Hall, and are publicly displayed, often in public lavatories. The disease is curable in the early stages, before permanent damage is done, by the use of penicillin. No one who suspects infection should ever hesitate to seek treatment for fear he can't be helped, because he can.

Genital Warts

These are little lumpy 'spots' which appear on the penis or vulva, which although they do little harm to men, may in some women cause cancer of the cervix, the opening to the uterus. They are not hard to remove, and always should be shown to a doctor if they appear.

Gonorrhea

This is spread in the same way as syphilis, and is also extremely unpleasant.

The first symptom is a severe inflammation of the sex organs, leading to a thick yellow foul discharge, either from the vagina or the penis. Also, there is often severe pain on passing water, especially in men.

The infection can spread to cause peritonitis, septicaemia (generalised blood poisoning), acute arthritis, severe inflammation of the eyes, meningitis (inflammation of the lining of the brain) and heart inflammation.

It can eventually lead to sterility in the woman, or stricture in the male.

A child born of a mother suffering from gonorrhoea may have its eyes so damaged that permanent blindness results.

Once again, the disease can be cured by early and prompt use of penicillin.

Chlamydia

This is similar in many ways to gonorrhoea and poses the same risks, so it needs careful diagnosis and treatment at a sexually transmitted disease clinic.

Epilogue

Whether you chose to give the second section of this book to your child to read, or preferred only to read it yourself and then talk to him or her about it, you should by now have a good deal of information that you did not perhaps have before. It isn't complete information, of course. There is so much more that is now known about the fascinating subject of human sexuality than there used to be that you could read on the subject for years, and still go on discovering new facts. But there should be enough here for any parent to be able to give his or her child honest answers to the questions that arise, be that child four or fourteen.

But if your child comes up with a question to which you can't find the answer in these pages (and since children have a remarkable gift for asking the unexpected there will be plenty of times when this will happen!) there need be no loss of face for you, as a parent, to say, 'I don't know,' — as long as you are able to add 'But I know how to find out.' To help you find out, there is at the end of this book a list of useful organisations which can help you in your search for facts.

For the rest, as long as you, as an adult, don't feel that sex is something too disgusting, too nasty, too frightening to talk about, your child will come to no harm. As long as you can keep an open mind, be ready to consider new attitudes towards sexual behaviour in humans, and don't let yourself be swamped by the prejudices that ill-informed adults poured into your mind when you were young, your child will develop into a mature and sexually responsible, happy adult. Which is what every parent wants for every child.

Useful Addresses

Brook Advisory Centre
153a East Street,
London
SE17 2SD

National Marriage Guidance Council
Herbert Gray College,
Little Church Street,
Rugby,
Warwickshire.

Catholic Marriage Advisory Council
15, Lansdowne Road,
Holland Park,
London
W11

Jewish Marriage Council
23, Ravenshurst Avenue,
London
NW4 4EL

Family Planning Association
27-35, Mortimer Street,
London
W1N 7RJ

Health Education Council
78, New Oxford Street,
London
WC1A 1AH

List of Titles in the Series

Parents' Guide to Toilet Training
Clare Hyman

The ABZ of Vitamins and Miners
Earl Mindell

The Anti-Acne Book
Dr David Murray

Pocket Guide to Yoga for Weight Control
Brian Netscher

Pocket Guide to Back Pain
Anthony Reed

The Pocket Guide to Branded Foods
Alexandra Sherman

The Sodium Counter
Alexandra Sherman

Pocket Guide to Stress
Dr Dick Thomson

The Cholesterol Counter
Isabel Winckler